RICKY MARTIN

A Real-Life Reader Biography

Valerie Menard

Mitchell Lane Publishers, Inc.

P.O. Box 200 • Childs, Maryland 21916

Mitchell Lane
PUBLISHERS

Second Printing

Real-Life Reader Biographies

Selena	Robert Rodriguez	Mariah Carey	Rafael Palmeiro
Tommy Nuñez	Trent Dimas	Cristina Saralegui	Andres Galarraga
Oscar De La Hoya	Gloria Estefan	Jimmy Smits	Mary Joe Fernandez
Cesar Chavez	Chuck Norris	Sinbad	Paula Abdul
Vanessa Williams	Celine Dion	Mia Hamm	Sammy Sosa
Brandy	Michelle Kwan	Rosie O'Donnell	Shania Twain
Garth Brooks	Jeff Gordon	Mark McGwire	Salma Hayek
Sheila E.	Hollywood Hogan	**Ricky Martin**	Britney Spears
Arnold Schwarzenegger	Jennifer Lopez	Kobe Bryant	Derek Jeter
Steve Jobs	Sandra Bullock	Julia Roberts	Robin Williams
Jennifer Love Hewitt	Keri Russell	Sarah Michelle Gellar	Liv Tyler
Melissa Joan Hart	Drew Barrymore	Alicia Silverstone	Katie Holmes
Winona Ryder	Alyssa Milano		

Library of Congress Cataloging-in-Publication Data
Menard, Valerie.
    Ricky Martin/Valerie Menard.
        p. cm. — (A real-life reader biography)
    Includes discography (p.) and index.
    Summary: Profiles the life and career of the Latin pop star best known for his hit song "Livin' la Vida Loca."
        ISBN 1-58415-059-9
    1. Martin, Ricky Juvenile literature. 2. Singers—Latin America Biography Juvenile literature. [1. Martin, Ricky. 2. Singers. 3. Puerto Ricans Biography.] I. Title. II. Series.
ML3930.M328M46 2000
782.42164'092—dc21
[B]
                                                                                          99-40617
                                                                                              CIP

ABOUT THE AUTHOR: Valerie Menard has been an editor for *Hispanic* magazine since the magazine moved to Austin, Texas, in July 1994. Before joining the magazine, she was a managing editor of a bilingual weekly, *La Prensa*. Valerie writes from a Latino perspective and as an advocate for Latino causes. She is the author of several biographies for children including **Oscar De La Hoya, Salma Hayek,** and **Cristina Saralegui** (Mitchell Lane).

PHOTO CREDITS: p. 4 Milan Ryba/Globe Photos; p. 9 Ron Davis/Shooting Star; p. 11 Globe Photos; pp. 13, 14 Danny Field/Shooting Star; p. 19 Robert Milazzo/Corbis; p. 24, 28 Lisa Rose/Globe Photos; p. 29 Colin Braley/Archive Photos

ACKNOWLEDGMENTS: The following story has been thoroughly researched, and to the best of our knowledge, represents a true story. Though we try to authorize every biography that we publish, for various reasons, this is not always possible. This story is neither authorized nor endorsed by Ricky Martin or any of his representatives.

Table of Contents

Chapter 1
A Star is Born

With the 1999 release of his first album in English, the red-hot singer Ricky Martin became an instant superstar. In its first week in stores, his album sold 661,000 copies, making it the best debut ever by a Latino artist.

But hit songs and fast-selling records are not new to Ricky. His first four solo records sold 15 million copies to fans in 26 countries throughout Latin America, Asia, Europe, and Australia. His Grammy Award–winning record *Vuelve* went platinum (one million copies sold) in the U.S., outselling recent

Hit songs and fast-selling records are not new to Ricky.

albums by superstars like Van Halen and Phil Collins. Before his solo career, Ricky was a star in the teen pop band Menudo, and a familiar face to fans of the soap opera *General Hospital*.

Special from the beginning, Enrique Martin Morales was born on Christmas Eve, December 24, 1971, in San Juan, the capital of Puerto Rico. His father, Enrique Martin III, was a psychiatrist, while his mother, Nereida Morales, was an accountant. They lived in the section of San Juan known as Hato Rey.

Puerto Rico is a small island in the Caribbean Sea, just southeast of the United States. The official language of the island is Spanish. The island has been part of the United States since the Spanish American War of 1898. Puerto Rico is a commonwealth, which means that it does not have all the rights and privileges as one of the 50 U.S. states. However, the residents of Puerto Rico are full-fledged citizens of the United States.

Enrique Martin Morales was born on Christmas Eve, December 24, 1971.

Ricky's childhood was fairly tranquil. Even though his parents divorced when he was quite young, Martin was surrounded by love. He called several places home, living mostly with his father in the middle-class suburb of University Gardens in Puerto Rico and for months at a time with his mother and grandparents. Ricky has two older half-brothers, Angel and Fernando, through his mother, and two half-brothers, Daniel and Eric, and a half-sister, Vanessa, from his father's subsequent marriage. Ricky attended Colegio Sagrado Corazón, a bilingual Catholic grade school, and at one time, was an altar boy.

He showed an early attraction for being in front of an audience. Rather than play baseball, Ricky and his friends would put on theatrical shows in the streets. Many times, Ricky pretended to be a tree. With arms outstretched he would shout, "I am a tree and I give shade and oxygen to the planet." As a boy, Ricky also loved to go to the

Rather than play baseball, Ricky and his friends would put on theatrical shows in the streets.

movies. Among his favorite films were *Star Wars* and *Return of the Jedi*. Although he found the character of Jabba the Hutt impressive, the character six-year-old Ricky liked the most was Luke Skywalker.

Like most kids in Puerto Rico, Ricky liked whatever was on the radio. When he was growing up, it was rock bands like Journey and singers like David Bowie. The first albums he ever bought were by these artists. "In those days," he admits in a 1999 *USA Today* article, "Latin sounds were not hip for my generation."

Eventually, his mother got tired of hearing rock music around the house. Nereida Morales decided to take Ricky and his brothers and sisters to the concerts of Latin music stars like Celia Cruz and Tito Puente. She encouraged Ricky to appreciate his culture through his own music. Besides her love, this may have been Nereida's greatest gift to her son, a love of his culture and its music. "I always say, no matter where

"Latin sounds were not hip for my gener— ation," says Ricky.

you are, those [Latin] drumbeats will go into your body and will make you dance," he said in May of 1999. "I'm really proud of my culture and my people..."

Ricky's perfor-mances prove that his Latin rhythm will make you want to dance.

Chapter 2
Menudo

**Ricky
Martin
seemed
destined
for a
career in
show
business.**

Ricky Martin seemed destined for a career in show business. He even started working at age seven, making television commercials. But when he was twelve, he got his big break when he was accepted into the Puerto Rican singing group Menudo.

Menudo had been formed in 1977. A promoter named Edgardo Diaz Melendez put the group together when he realized that no Spanish-language group existed to appeal to young adults in Latin America. There were five members—two were sons of a friend of Diaz, and three were sons of one of his cousins. All the original members were Puerto Rican. In Puerto Rico, "menudo" means "little guy" or "small change."

The five members of Menudo varied in age from eleven to sixteen. From the beginning, Diaz set a rule that once a member turned seventeen, he would have to leave the group. This would help Menudo maintain its youthful appeal and its fan base, Diaz believed. He also wanted the members of Menudo to be clean-cut—no drugs, good grades, and a positive attitude.

When he was twelve, Ricky auditioned three times to be in Menudo. He was

There were five members of Menudo. Ricky is shown bottom left.

refused twice, but finally was accepted on the third try. Ricky would replace the last original member of the band, Ricky Melendez. Ricky Martin joined the group on July 10, 1984.

"He was small, not a big singer, and his voice was not so good then," Edgardo Diaz Melendez later said. "But we thought he could learn a lot by being with the group."

The group's manager was not the only one to have doubts about Ricky at first. His fellow Menudo singers were also a little concerned. "I always remember the first night [Ricky] went on stage with us at the Centro de Bellas Artes in San Juan," former bandmate Charlie Masso recalled. "He was very, very shy, and we were concerned about how he was going to react on stage, but he immediately caught on."

Being part of Menudo was a mixed blessing. Ricky gained important experience, but it came at a price. He had to grow up a lot faster than most twelve year olds and he spent a lot of

> **Being part of Menudo was a mixed blessing. He gained important experience, but it came at a price.**

time away from his family. As Martin describes it, "One day I was riding a bicycle and the next day, I was performing in front of an audience of 200,000 people."

Even after all the singing and dancing lessons that Ricky took to

Ricky was twelve years old when he was accepted to be a part of the teen group Menudo.

prepare for concerts, the crowd was pretty scary. But once it was over, all he wanted to do was get back on stage. Today, he still loves it. "Being on stage, it's just . . . ahhhhh, you know?" he told *USA Today.* "I was born for this. I don't want to sound too dramatic, but I want to die on stage."

Despite this, Ricky Martin will admit to being very shy. It's when he's on stage that he can let go and show off. As he explains: "I'm a very reserved person and it's difficult for me to express myself. . . . I need the stage to rid myself of all my insecurities. When I'm onstage I am Superman."

When Ricky first got on stage, he was shy. But, soon, he learned how to show off.

But life in Menudo was never easy. The boys rehearsed every day. They were only allowed a few hours each day for recreation and education. Since the group was constantly touring, Diaz had arranged for them to have personal tutors so that they would not fall behind in school. "Menudo was my school," Martin later said. "I'm very proud of those beginnings. Menudo taught me the true meaning of the word Discipline, and every time I write that word, I capitalize it."

Traveling and performing were especially hard on Ricky's family life. He was not even allowed to leave the tour for a few days to attend his grandfather's funeral. And his parents, who had divorced before he was three, began to compete for their son's attention. At one point, Ricky's father asked him to choose which parent he preferred. Ricky was so hurt by this that he refused to speak to his father for ten years. He told both parents at the time that to ask a child to choose between parents was terrible. It wasn't until Martin joined the cast of *General Hospital* in 1994 that he made an effort to forgive his father.

Ricky also had two life-threatening experiences on the concert circuit. He survived a bad car wreck in Argentina,

Traveling and performing were especially hard on Ricky's family life.

where his car actually flipped, and one time after he had just gotten off a plane in San Diego, it took off, ran out of fuel, and crashed.

But a lot of good did come out of his experience in Menudo. One important thing was that Martin met his best friend, Robi Rosa. They were roommates while in the band. Today, Rosa co-writes songs with Martin and produces his records. "We speak the same language," says Martin about Rosa. "I tell him what I'm feeling, and he translates that to words and music and then I take that to the stage and make it work."

Ricky Martin also learned a lot while in Menudo. He stayed with the band for five years. During that time he traveled all over the world, to places like Italy, Japan, Guam, Spain, and all of Latin America. The years that Ricky Martin spent with Menudo may have been tough, but at least he was well-paid. He was a millionaire by the time he left the group at age seventeen.

While a member of Menudo, Ricky met his best friend, Robi Rosa. Today, Rosa co-writes songs with Martin.

Chapter 3
Life After Menudo

When Ricky left Menudo in 1989, he decided that he had earned enough money to take some time off and not work for a while. He decided to finish high school. Once he graduated, he moved to New York City and spent eight months exploring the city. Then he moved to Mexico City, where his acting career began to develop.

He starred in several Mexican soap operas (these are called *telenovelas*), including *Alcanzar una Estrella II* ("To Reach for a Star"). Ricky won the Heraldo, the highest award in Mexico given for acting, for his performance in

When Ricky left Menudo, he took some time off for himself.

Ricky was offered a part on the soap opera, *General Hospital*. He played Miguel Morez, a hospital orderly and bartender.

a movie version of this *telenovela*. At the same time, he began a solo music career, performing in the musical *Mamá Ama el Rock* ("Mama Loves Rock") and signing a record deal with Sony Discos, the Mexican division of Sony Records. His first album, *Ricky Martin*, was released in 1991. He followed this up with a second record, *Me Amarás*, in 1993.

As his popularity grew in Mexico, Ricky was noticed by an executive with the popular American soap opera *General Hospital*. Martin's manager, Ricardo Cordero, sent videos and records to the network and invited them to see him perform live. The executives were convinced that he had appeal, but they were not sure he could act. They asked Ricky to audition.

Ricky looked great at the audition, and was immediately offered a job on *General Hospital*. He would play Miguel Morez, a hospital orderly and bartender who would be called upon to sing on certain occasions. He wore long hair and was paired with actress Lily Melgar, who played Miguel's first love.

In interviews, most soap opera actors say that acting is hard work. They have to memorize new lines every day, rehearse, and then tape a scene until it is right. This can keep them at the studio all day. But Ricky Martin was used to the grind from his days with Menudo, and he welcomed the challenge. In an interview shortly after he took the soap-opera job in 1994, Ricky commented, "For me, *General Hospital* has been an incredible way of learning and growing as an actor. I look at it as a training school that's going to help my acting career. I think it will even help me

When Ricky appeared on General Hospital, *he wore his hair long.*

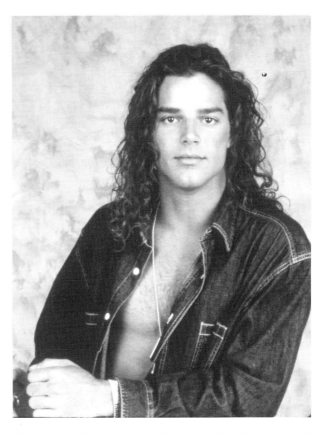

in my musical career. At concerts I'm always in front of the public, and acting gives you more self-confidence."

Even though his role on *General Hospital* kept him busy, Ricky continued to sing. He occasionally performed in the U.S., even selling out a show at Radio City Music Hall in New York City. He was starting to draw a lot of attention. Ricky was asked to provide the voice for Hercules in the Spanish version of Disney's animated movie. He also recorded his third album, *A Medio Vivir*. When the album was released in 1995, Ricky's song "Maria" became his biggest hit to date.

As sales of *A Medio Vivir* began to explode, Martin felt the need to promote the record in a concert tour. In January 1996 he left *General Hospital*. The tour took him several places including the U.S. where he started to get attention from the media. In one interview, he mentioned that he had always dreamed of performing in the theaters on New York City's Broadway. When the

> **Even though his role on *General Hospital* kept him busy, he continued to sing.**

executive producer of a popular show titled *Les Miserables* happened to read the story, he called Ricky with a job offer. "It doesn't matter what I do, I'll do it," Martin told the producer.

Les Miserables is based on a novel written by Victor Hugo. It is the story of two couples who are caught up in the devastation of the French Revolution in the 19th century. Martin moved back to New York for his appearance on Broadway. He joined the cast of *Les Miserables* for the tenth anniversary of the show's opening, playing the role of Marius.

Ricky joined the cast of *Les Miserables* on Broadway for the tenth anniver—sary of the show's opening.

Chapter 4
The Grammys

By 1999, Ricky Martin was a superstar in Latin America, and was ready to take off in the United States as well. It only took two performances: one during the Grammy Awards ceremony on February 26, and the other on the television program *Saturday Night Live* on May 6.

The Grammy Awards, presented each year by the National Association of Recording Arts and Sciences (NARAS), are considered the highest honor given to musicians in the U.S. However, for many years, there was only one music category to recognize Latino musicians,

In 1999, Ricky performed at the Grammys.

22

the Latin Pop Album category. Eventually, NARAS began to recognize the influence and popularity of Latino music and expanded the categories to include Mexican-American Album, Latin Jazz Album, Latin Rock or Alternative Album, Tropical Latin Album, and Tejano Album. It was in the Latin Pop category, however, that Martin received his first Grammy nomination. His fourth album, *Vuelve*, had been released in 1998 and was so well-regarded that Ricky was asked to perform at the show.

This was a special accomplishment. The Grammy Awards ceremony is an all-night affair, and the entire show is not televised. Latin performers like Gloria Estefan, Arturo Sandoval, and the popular Tejano singer Selena have not always appeared during the prime-time telecast. But in 1999, show organizers became convinced that Ricky Martin would improve the show.

Another Latino entertainer, actor/singer Jennifer Lopez, appreciates the

Latin performers do not always appear during the prime-time broadcast.

rare chance Martin received to perform on the Grammys, "A few years ago, you might not have seen a Latin Pop Album award being presented on the Grammys," she says.

Ricky planned to sing his hit "La Copa de la Vida," ("The Cup of Life"). This song had been chosen by the World Cup Soccer Federation as the official

Ricky, with his girlfriend, at the 1999 Grammys.

anthem for its 1998 World Cup championship. Ricky was excited and nervous. This was his chance to show a room full of music stars and record executives just what he had to offer. He organized fifteen musicians and fifteen dancers to perform with him and rehearsed with them for four days. "I was anxious at the Grammys," Ricky later told *Entertainment Weekly*. "So I said, 'Dude, you've been doing this for fifteen years. Just be yourself.'"

All his hard work paid off. His performance not only featured Latin rhythms, but a Ricky Martin that was full of energy and enthusiasm. The audience at the ceremony found the performance irresistible. When Ricky finished, the crowd stood up to clap and cheer—the only standing ovation by any artist that night. To cap off a great night, Ricky also took home the award for Best Latin Pop Album, which was presented to him by Gloria Estefan and actor Jimmy Smits.

After the show, John Lannert, the Latin American music editor of *Billboard* magazine, praised Ricky's performance. "You're at the Grammies, you've already seen Madonna and a couple of other acts perform and it's same-old, same-old," Lannert wrote. "Then Martin comes up with 30 people. He's the epitome of 'timing is everything.' He's at the right place, at the right time with the right sound." This sound is sometimes called Latin pop, or referred

Ricky's song, "La Copa de la Vida" had been chosen by the World Cup Federation as the official anthem for its 1998 World Cup championship.

to as "fusion" because it combines rock, pop, and Latin music.

Thanks to the Grammy appearance, people were ready when Ricky's first English-language single was released in April. "Livin' la Vida Loca," rocketed up the *Billboard* charts, reaching number one by the beginning of May. The song spent the next several weeks at the top of the charts. After the video to the song premiered on MTV, it became the most requested video in the music channel's history.

As his popularity began to grow, Ricky was booked to perform on the television program *Saturday Night Live*. More than ten million people tuned in to the May 6 show—29 percent more viewers than usual. It was the biggest *Saturday Night Live* audience of the season.

Suddenly, Ricky Martin was officially a superstar, and was being called "sexy," "heartthrob," "phenomenon," "sensational," and "electrifying."

Fusion combines rock, pop, and Latin music.

Chapter 5
Crossover
Record

Before the May 1999 release of *Ricky Martin*, Ricky's four previous solo records had already sold a combined 15 million copies in Latin America, Asia, Europe, and Australia. But the new album hit the U.S. charts hard, because it appealed to both English-speaking and Spanish-speaking fans. *Ricky Martin* debuted at number one, and stayed at the top of the album charts for more than three months. From the start, Ricky knew he had a hit. "With all humbleness, I think we'll sell 10 million copies, " he told *Entertainment Weekly*.

From the start, Ricky knew he had a hit.

With all the attention, it was almost a sure thing that the second single from *Ricky Martin*, "She's All I Ever Had," would be a hit. The album also features the song Ricky performed at the Grammys, "The Cup of Life," as well as a duet with pop superstar Madonna titled "Cuidado Con Mi Corazon" ("Be Careful"). To promote *Ricky Martin*, the singer announced that he would tour the United States, beginning in October. When word of the 16-city concert tour got out, fans got into line for tickets. Shows in 20,000-seat arenas sold out in a matter of minutes.

"You'll have the Latin touch. You'll be dancing a lot in the show, definitely," Ricky told MTV

Ricky appeared in Tower Records in California to promote the release of "Livin' La Vida Loca."

News. "We're, like, 15 people on stage. We're talking an amazing band. People that I've worked with for many years. People that know the real meaning of the word fusion. And that's exactly what we want to share with the audience."

Of course his success has been sweet—"It's addictive," Ricky admits.

On April 23, 1999, Ricky released his first English-language album. Below, he enters a Miami Beach music store for a record signing.

But the young singer always remains aware of the new ground that he is breaking for other Latino artists, just as guitarist Carlos Santana and singer Gloria Estefan did for him. Martin's success has helped focus attention on the new trend in music called Latin pop.

Although the attention may be great, it can also be overwhelming. To release the pressure, Ricky likes to exercise. He works out every day and even rock climbs. To this exercise regimen he adds yoga and meditation.

His manner of dressing matches his philosophy on life. He knows he has to look good in public—his favorite designer is Armani—but at home in Miami Ricky prefers to be comfortable, wearing pajamas most of the time.

In the future, Ricky would like to try

Ricky can put on quite a performance! He's had 15 years of practice on stage.

acting in the movies someday. He also says that he would like to try performing on Broadway again. For now, though, he's enjoying the moment while trying not to let it get to him. "It's very seductive to be part of that wave [of fame] and I've felt it," he says. "You start feeling that grandiosity complex and it becomes part of you and then you think you're God and you deserve it all . . . That's not good for you." At age 27, he has learned to put fame in its proper place—after his family, his friends, and himself.

"I'm taking it one day at a time," Ricky admits. "I want to do this for a long time, and for that to happen, you've got to keep things as simple as they can get."

"I'm taking it one day at a time," Ricky admits.

Discography

Ricky Martin (Sony Discos, 1991)
Me Amarás (Sony Discos, 1993)
A Medio Vivir (Sony Discos, 1995)
Vuelve (Sony Discos, 1998)
Ricky Martin (Columbia, 1999)

Chronology

1971 Enrique "Ricky" Martin Morales born in Hato Rey, Puerto Rico, on December 24.
1984 Ricky Martin joins the teen pop band Menudo on July 10.
1989 Leaves the band and takes time off to finish high school; lives in New York City.
1991 Finds work on a Mexican soap opera while living in Mexico City; signs a record contract with Sony Discos; releases first record, *Ricky Martin*.
1994 Moves to Los Angeles and joins the cast of the ABC soap opera *General Hospital.*
1996 Scores first hit single, "Maria," from his third album, *A Medio Vivir;* joins the cast of *Les Miserables* on Broadway in June.
1998 Releases fourth album, *Vuelve*, which is nominated for a Grammy Award.
1999 Performs at the Grammy Award ceremony on February 24, overwhelming the audience, and takes home a Grammy Award for Best Latin Pop Album; releases the hit single "Livin' la Vida Loca" in April; first English-language album, *Ricky Martin,* is released in May; begins U.S. concert tour in October.

Index